MORE...
how to continue your Evolution for Success.

Volume I

January-June

James M. Murphy

Copyright © 2015 James M Murphy

All rights reserved.

ISBN:1503170365
ISBN-13:9781503170360

DEDICATION

This book is dedicated the those human souls who hunger for something more, who strive to become a little bit better everyday and in the end-
Change The World.

And to my son, Nicolas.
I am proud of the man you are becoming on your path to being and achieving MORE!

HOW TO ACHIEVE... MORE!

MORE...

I guarantee that right now, in some area of your life, you want MORE of something. Even if you just answered that statement with, "James, everything in my life is just perfect, couldn't be better!" Try this quick experiment.

"Stop, sit, close your eyes, relax, breathe and just be present in the moment for as long as you can." How long did you make it? Do you remember feeling that moment when you just HAD to open you eyes, get up and start moving. That is the moment of wanting MORE. Even the most focused meditator will eventually have to get up and do something.

So the question is, "what do you want MORE of?" Most people know what they don't want MORE of: yard work, dishes, bills, work, and people telling them what they should, could and must do.

Or maybe you do know what you want MORE of: money, cars, time, clothes, shoes, time at the beach, travel, happiness, love, knowledge, fun or freedom.

No matter what you want MORE of there are only two ways you are going to get it; by life's events impacting you or by you choosing to take action towards what you want MORE of.

The most effective way to have MORE in life is to be a purposeful person. Purposeful people build and create incredible emotional experiences that move, motivate and inspire themselves to continually take actions towards the completion of their goals.

That begs the question. How does a person become Purposeful? Purpose is attained through the power found in the acronym F.O.C.U.S.S.

A person is Purposeful when they Focus On Creating a Unique Self and Skill. Notice the order: Self, then Skill. By tackling a goal that is genuinely meaningful to them, as opposed to one that is defined by others, they have a solid sense of purpose that fuels them moving forward.

This workbook is for you to write down every day what you are going to do to move toward your purposeful, focused goals. By taking a few minutes each day to focus on your end goal, you will move purposefully forward, instead of getting lost in a flurry of actions that may not yield significant results. It will keep you motivated, and in turn, will inspire more consistent, focused actions.

I am living proof that the process of writing down what you want in life and committing to doing something towards it every day works.

In 1991, I graduated college with a degree in Economics from Iowa State and couldn't find a job. So, I enlisted the US Army Infantry and ended up in the Honor Guard, 3rd US Infantry, in Arlington, VA. I went on to be a squad leader for a full honor casket team and earned my Airborne, Air Assault, and Expert Infantry Badges. My humblest and most honorable moments were the days I marched at the

Tomb of the Unknown Soldier and presented our nations flag to next of kin in honor the selfless service and sacrifice of a fallen brother.

In 1996, out of over 17,000 applicants, I was one of less than 100 people to graduate from the Federal Law Enforcement training center as a Deputy United States Marshal. I was assigned to Denver, Colorado and participated in the Oklahoma City Bombing Trials involving Timothy McVey and Terry Nichols.

In 1999, I resigned to go work for one of the world's most dynamic, motivational speakers, Anthony Robbins. In the next 10 years, I immersed myself in helping others create results in their lives and logged over 25,000 coaching sessions. In 2010, I started my own Executive Coaching Business, Evolution for Success.

In 2008, my wife and I were able to purchase our brand new home mortgage free.

In one calendar year, from April 2010-11, I ran a multitude of races that included 4 marathons, a 40, 50, and 62 mile ultramarathon, and I topped it all off by completing the Umstead 100 Mile Ultra Marathon.

At this point, you are either impressed or saying, "What a bragger," (or both). The truth is, I'm just an "an ordinary Iowa boy."

How does success and having MORE in life happen? By accepting the fact that every success comes with obstacles that will need to be overcome.

My bedroom in our old farmhouse had a built-in room heater and in the winter, the pilot light would blow out and I would be without heat. During the humid summers, my sisters and I slept on the living room floor because we only had one window AC unit in the house. We never went hungry, but we shopped at the day old bread store. SPAM and bologna sandwiches were common.

I worked 75 hours a week every summer to pay for my college education. During the day, I worked as a janitor at a steel mill and later had to clean outhouses at a county park. At night and on weekends, I worked my way up from dishwasher to line cook at an Italian Restaurant.

I was on academic probation in college just about as many semesters than not, and barely graduated. I had to drop 60 lbs to get into the military. When I left the service I moved across the country with everything I owned in the back of my car and $900 to my name. As I waited through the year and a half it took to get through the hiring process for the US Marshal Service, I had to live with friends and find whatever work I could. And even after I left the Marshal Service and started working for Tony Robbins in San Diego, the stock market tanked, business dried up, and again I had to go back to living paycheck to paycheck. Finally, I was rejected dozens of times as I worked to establish my own full time coaching practice, and was told after suffering a knee injury I should never run again

However, my work with Robbins had made a tremendous impact on my way of looking at both struggles and success. It gave me an opportunity to see what strategies consistently worked to overcome obstacles to success. The one presented in the 6 month journal is the first success strategy I learned.

Ultimately, what fueled my resolve to push forward past the obstacles to reach my goals —whether it was a thriving Executive Coaching practice, a mortgage free home, or completing a 100 mile ultra-marathon— was ***being emotionally connected to my outcomes, writing them down, committing to them, and then consistently, relentlessly, and purposefully taking action in the direction I wanted to go.***

One of my greatest successes was finishing my 100 Mile Ultra Marathon. But I actually completed the race at mile 95, not 100. At that point, I was physically drained, mentally and emotionally exhausted and all I could think of was uttering the words, "I Quit." In that moment, I had a choice to either give up or move forward and connect with the inner part of me that wanted MORE for myself. I chose to take that next step forward.

Most people fail in life because they don't have the staying power to keep moving forward no matter what the cost. In the end, most people just give up way too soon. In our modern society, people have a hard time staying focused for 2-3 minutes, much less 2-3 months or the 2-3 years it may take to really build and create something amazing. If a person can not give their word to write down 3-5 specific actions they are committed to take every day to achieve their goals and follow through, "how bad do they want it?"

Being Purposeful is a MUST if you want MORE.

Three things link all of my successes.

1. They were all *personal* pursuits that I chose to pursue to make ME a better person on the inside.

2. They were all long term goals that were way bigger than me, and took more than a day, week, or month to accomplish.

3. I wrote down what I was committed to achieving every day and never quit.

Success and having MORE in life is ALWAYS about how you lived and the choices you made during the days, months, and even years, prior to that moment it became real.

Tony Robbins once said, "most people overestimate what they can do in a year but underestimate what they can accomplish in ten." I agree!

Find the pleasure in getting a little better and experiencing a little MORE every day!

To your continued success,

James

HOW TO USE THIS BOOK FOR MORE...

Q: What one thing I can build and create in my life that will allow me to Focus On Creating a Unique Self and Skill?
A:

_____

_____

Will it: also allow me to build and create an incredible emotional experience for myself ?   Y   N

Will it allow me to build and create an incredible emotional experience for others that will move others to do the same in their lives?   Y   N

Will this goal give me a chance to build and create a more unique "Self?"   Y   N

Will this goal give me a chance to build and create a unique "Skill?"   Y   N

Is this a long term goal that will take at least a year to achieve?   Y   N

Do you think, "Am I a little a crazy for attempting this?"   Y   N

Do your closest family, friends, neighbors and co-workers think you are just a little crazy?   Y   N

If the answers were all "Y" then you are good to go. If any answer was a "N" then start over.
Everyday, review the following Goals Page.

Next, there are three options for filling in the #1-5.

Option 1:
Pick one thing you will do every day to Mentally, Emotionally, Physically, Spiritually and Financially move towards your MORE goal. List one per line.
1. Mental: Strengthen your Beliefs, Visualizations and Thoughts.
2. Emotional: Emotionally associate to your goals, feel how it will feel to achieve it.
3. Physical: List the specific action will you take to move towards the goal (what you fear or are procrastinating the most is a good place to start)
4. Spiritual: Write down what you can have trust and faith in so that you strengthen the belief you will accomplish the goal (or just pray!)
5.Financial: Take an action to financially invest in whatever it takes to achieve your goal (not just spending money, it could be saving money, checking your account balances, anything to be financially responsible to achieve the goal).

Option 2:
Pick the top 3 actions you are committed to do each day in order to move towards the long term MORE goal.

To determine these I sometimes ask myself, "What are the top things I need to accomplish today, so that if I died and went to heaven at the end of the day, I would die a whole and complete man?"

Option 3:

If you want to use the book to build and create new habits in the pursuit of MORE, remember that a habit has three main parts.

1. There is a Trigger. A trigger is an action that sets off a "set or sequence of actions" that produces a desired or undesired result. There is a reason that all of the candy bars are right at the checkout line in the store. Once you "see" the candy, that may be all it takes to set off the trigger.

2. The trigger causes you to unconsciously act. Part two is the Action. Once you see that candy bar, the unconscious association to it is engaged and you ACT, picking it up and putting it on the tail end of the groceries on the conveyer belt.

3. Last is the Reward! Oh, how good it tastes to sit in the car after such a long stressful grocery shopping day, enjoying the silence and munching down on that nice, sweet treat!

Use your Lines 1-3 on each daily checklist and list a new: Trigger (1) - Action (2) - Reward (3) sequence to build your new MORE habit. It will have to be conscious at first but with repetition and time, your behaviors will change to have a more positive result.

TWO LAST POINTS:

1. Never go to bed without checking off everything on your daily MORE list!

2. If you miss a day, FORGIVE yourself and continue on!

MORE...

MY PRIMARY GOAL FOR THE YEAR IS TO BUILD & CREATE...

_____

_____

_____

MY QUARTERLY OUTCOMES TO BUILD AND CREATE THIS GOAL ARE...

Q1._____

Q2._____

Q3._____

Q4._____

JANUARY 1

Today, I am absolutely committed to Be, Do and Have more in my life. Before I go to sleep tonight I give my word to...

_____
#1

_____
#2

_____
#3

_____
#4

_____
#5

_____

"To change one's life: start immediately; do it flamboyantly, no exceptions." ~William James

JANUARY 2

Today, I am absolutely committed to Be, Do and Have more in my life. Before I go to sleep tonight I give my word to...

#1

#2

#3

#4

#5

"Find the Joy in that moment you find yourself getting just a little bit better." ~James Murphy

JANUARY 3

Today, I am absolutely committed to Be, Do and Have more in my life. Before I go to sleep tonight I give my word to...

#1

#2

#3

#4

#5

"The way to get started is to quit talking and begin doing." ~Walt Disney Company

JANUARY 4

Today, I am absolutely committed to Be, Do and Have more in my life. Before I go to sleep tonight I give my word to...

#1

#2

#3

#4

#5

"Love yourself more than anything."
~James Murphy

JANUARY 5

Today, I am absolutely committed to Be, Do and Have more in my life. Before I go to sleep tonight I give my word to...

#1

#2

#3

#4

#5

"Show the world you are crazy. Set a goal that makes others doubt, laugh and disbelieve."   ~James Murphy

JANUARY 6

Today, I am absolutely committed to Be, Do and Have more in my life. Before I go to sleep tonight I give my word to...

_____
#1

_____
#2

_____
#3

_____
#4

_____
#5

_____

"The quickest path to confidence lies in keeping your word with yourself and others."   ~James M Murphy

JANUARY 7

Today, I am absolutely committed to Be, Do and Have more in my life. Before I go to sleep tonight I give my word to...

#1

#2

#3

#4

#5

"Sometimes it takes a good fall to really know where you stand." ~Hayley Williams

JANUARY 8

Today, I am absolutely committed to Be, Do and Have more in my life. Before I go to sleep tonight I give my word to...

#1

#2

#3

#4

#5

"It's always worthwhile to let others know of their worth." ~Malcolm Forbes

JANUARY 9

Today, I am absolutely committed to Be, Do and Have more in my life. Before I go to sleep tonight I give my word to...

#1

#2

#3

#4

#5

"Your success in life is directly proportional to the amount of risk and uncertainty you can manage."
~Anthony Robbins

JANUARY 10

Today, I am absolutely committed to Be, Do and Have more in my life. Before I go to sleep tonight I give my word to...

#1

#2

#3

#4

#5

"It is hard to fail, but its worse to never have tried to succeed."   ~Theodore Roosevelt

JANUARY 11

Today, I am absolutely committed to Be, Do and Have more in my life. Before I go to sleep tonight I give my word to...

_____
#1

_____
#2

_____
#3

_____
#4

_____
#5

_____

"Success is most often achieved by those who don't know that failure is inevitable."   ~CoCo Chanel

JANUARY 12

Today, I am absolutely committed to Be, Do and Have more in my life. Before I go to sleep tonight I give my word to...

#1

#2

#3

#4

#5

"When I started running, 2 miles nearly killed me. Twenty years later...I killed that 100-mile course!"
~James M Murphy

JANUARY 13

Today, I am absolutely committed to Be, Do and Have more in my life. Before I go to sleep tonight I give my word to...

#1

#2

#3

#4

#5

"A thinker see his own actions as experiments and questions--as attempts to find out something. Success and failure are for him answers above all."
~Friedrich Nietzsche

JANUARY 14

Today, I am absolutely committed to Be, Do and Have more in my life. Before I go to sleep tonight I give my word to...

_____
#1

_____
#2

_____
#3

_____
#4

_____
#5

_____

"Only those who dare to fail greatly can ever achieve greatly." ~Robert F. Kennedy

JANUARY 15

Today, I am absolutely committed to Be, Do and Have more in my life. Before I go to sleep tonight I give my word to...

#1

#2

#3

#4

#5

"Today change from impossible, to I'm Possible."
~James M Murphy

JANUARY 16

Today, I am absolutely committed to Be, Do and Have more in my life. Before I go to sleep tonight I give my word to...

_____
#1

_____
#2

_____
#3

_____
#4

_____
#5

_____

"Kites rise highest against the wind, not with it."
~Winston S. Churchill

JANUARY 17

Today, I am absolutely committed to Be, Do and Have more in my life. Before I go to sleep tonight I give my word to...

#1

#2

#3

#4

#5

"Make a pact with yourself today not to be defined by your past." ~Steve Maraboli

JANUARY 18

Today, I am absolutely committed to Be, Do and Have more in my life. Before I go to sleep tonight I give my word to...

#1

#2

#3

#4

#5

"When you do what you fear most, you can do anything." ~Stephen Richards

JANUARY 19

Today, I am absolutely committed to Be, Do and Have more in my life. Before I go to sleep tonight I give my word to...

#1

#2

#3

#4

#5

"Be Bold, Be Fearless, Be the Power that lies within your soul." ~James Murphy

JANUARY 20

Today, I am absolutely committed to Be, Do and Have more in my life. Before I go to sleep tonight I give my word to...

#1

#2

#3

#4

#5

"The difference between a successful person and others is not a lack of strength, not a lack of knowledge, but rather a lack in will." ~Vince Lombardi

JANUARY 21

Today, I am absolutely committed to Be, Do and Have more in my life. Before I go to sleep tonight I give my word to...

#1

#2

#3

#4

#5

"Forget yesterday - it has already forgotten you. Don't sweat tomorrow - you haven't even met. Open your eyes and hear to today." ~Steve Maraboli

JANUARY 22

Today, I am absolutely committed to Be, Do and Have more in my life. Before I go to sleep tonight I give my word to...

#1

#2

#3

#4

#5

"When in an unresourceful emotional state...STOP, sit with the feeling, understand the conflict inside, learn what you need to learn to let it go. Then open yourself up and ask for the clear next step and take action."

~James Murphy

JANUARY 23

Today, I am absolutely committed to Be, Do and Have more in my life. Before I go to sleep tonight I give my word to...

#1

#2

#3

#4

#5

"Success comes from listening to your conscience and being dedicated to purposeful action, in the moment and in the long run."   ~James Murphy

JANUARY 24

Today, I am absolutely committed to Be, Do and Have more in my life. Before I go to sleep tonight I give my word to...

#1

#2

#3

#4

#5

"We are all failures, at least the best of us are."
~J.M. Barrie

JANUARY 25

Today, I am absolutely committed to Be, Do and Have more in my life. Before I go to sleep tonight I give my word to...

#1

#2

#3

#4

#5

"Whatever the mind of a man can conceive and believe, it can achieve.."   ~Napolean Hill

JANUARY 26

Today, I am absolutely committed to Be, Do and Have more in my life. Before I go to sleep tonight I give my word to...

_____
#1

_____
#2

_____
#3

_____
#4

_____
#5

_____

"Always bear in mind that your resolution to succeed is more important than anything."   ~Abraham Lincoln

JANUARY 27

Today, I am absolutely committed to Be, Do and Have more in my life. Before I go to sleep tonight I give my word to...

#1

#2

#3

#4

#5

"Our greatest fear should not be of failure but of succeeding at things in life that don't really matter."
~Francis Chan

JANUARY 28

Today, I am absolutely committed to Be, Do and Have more in my life. Before I go to sleep tonight I give my word to...

_____
#1

_____
#2

_____
#3

_____
#4

_____
#5

_____

"Supreme excellence consists of breaking the enemy's resistance without fighting." ~Sun Tzu

JANUARY 29

Today, I am absolutely committed to Be, Do and Have more in my life. Before I go to sleep tonight I give my word to...

_____
#1

_____
#2

_____
#3

_____
#4

_____
#5

_____

"When you show yourself to the world and display your talents, you naturally stir all kinds of resentment, envy and other manifestations of insecurity...you can not spend your life worrying about the petty feelings of others."
~Robert Green

JANUARY 30

Today, I am absolutely committed to Be, Do and Have more in my life. Before I go to sleep tonight I give my word to...

#1

#2

#3

#4

#5

"Never confuse your decisions with your identity; who you think you are. Success is making mistakes. What you learn from them determines your identity."

~James Murphy

JANUARY 31

Today, I am absolutely committed to Be, Do and Have more in my life. Before I go to sleep tonight I give my word to...

#1

#2

#3

#4

#5

"It's the end of the month; review, recognize and reward your positive results."   ~James Murphy

IN JANUARY, I CREATED MORE...

FEBRUARY 1

Today, I am absolutely committed to Be, Do and Have more in my life. Before I go to sleep tonight I give my word to...

#1

#2

#3

#4

#5

"One of the biggest challenges of success is to balance staying confident yet humble, focused on creating MORE and approaching others with a servant heart.."
~James Murphy

FEBRUARY 2

Today, I am absolutely committed to Be, Do and Have more in my life. Before I go to sleep tonight I give my word to...

_____
#1

_____
#2

_____
#3

_____
#4

_____
#5

_____

"I've had great success being a total idiot."
~Jerry Lewis

FEBRUARY 3

Today, I am absolutely committed to Be, Do and Have more in my life. Before I go to sleep tonight I give my word to...

#1

#2

#3

#4

#5

"Success does not consist in never making mistakes but in never making the same one a second time."
~George Bernard Shaw

FEBRUARY 4

Today, I am absolutely committed to Be, Do and Have more in my life. Before I go to sleep tonight I give my word to...

#1

#2

#3

#4

#5

"The three great essentials to achieve anything worthwhile are, first, hard work, second, stick-to-itiveness; third, common sense." ~Thomas Edison

FEBRUARY 5

Today, I am absolutely committed to Be, Do and Have more in my life. Before I go to sleep tonight I give my word to...

_____
#1

_____
#2

_____
#3

_____
#4

_____
#5

_____

"And will you succeed? Yes indeed, yes indeed! Ninety-eight and three-quarters percent guaranteed!." ~Dr. Seuss

FEBRUARY 6

Today, I am absolutely committed to Be, Do and Have more in my life. Before I go to sleep tonight I give my word to...

#1

#2

#3

#4

#5

"In order to succeed, your desire for success should be greater than your fear of failure."   ~Bill Cosby

FEBRUARY 7

Today, I am absolutely committed to Be, Do and Have more in my life. Before I go to sleep tonight I give my word to...

#1

#2

#3

#4

#5

"Eighty percent of success is showing up!"
~Woody Allen

FEBRUARY 8

Today, I am absolutely committed to Be, Do and Have more in my life. Before I go to sleep tonight I give my word to...

#1

#2

#3

#4

#5

"Judge your success by what you have to give up in order to get it."   ~Dalai Lama XIV

FEBRUARY 9

Today, I am absolutely committed to Be, Do and Have more in my life. Before I go to sleep tonight I give my word to...

_____
#1

_____
#2

_____
#3

_____
#4

_____
#5

_____

"Walk with the dreamers, the believers, the courageous, the cheerful, the planners, the doers, the successful people with their heads in the clouds and their fee on the ground. Let their spirit ignite a fire within you to leave this world better than when you found it..."   ~Wilfred Peterson

FEBRUARY 10

Today, I am absolutely committed to Be, Do and Have more in my life. Before I go to sleep tonight I give my word to...

_____
#1

_____
#2

_____
#3

_____
#4

_____
#5

_____

"To each there comes in their lifetime a special moment when they are figuratively tapped on the shoulder and offered a chance to do a very special thing, unique to them and fitted to their talents. What a tragedy if that moment finds them unprepared or unqualified for that which could have been their finest hour."
~Winston S. Churchill

FEBRUARY 11

Today, I am absolutely committed to Be, Do and Have more in my life. Before I go to sleep tonight I give my word to...

#1

#2

#3

#4

#5

"Success is getting what you want. Happiness is wanting what you get." ~Dale Carnegie

FEBRUARY 12

Today, I am absolutely committed to Be, Do and Have more in my life. Before I go to sleep tonight I give my word to...

#1

#2

#3

#4

#5

"Love, nurture and grow yourself so you can most help others to love, grow and become their best self."
~James Murphy

FEBRUARY 13

Today, I am absolutely committed to Be, Do and Have more in my life. Before I go to sleep tonight I give my word to...

_____
#1

_____
#2

_____
#3

_____
#4

_____
#5

_____

"You create your life and the exact amount of success you deserve." ~James Murphy

FEBRUARY 14

Today, I am absolutely committed to Be, Do and Have more in my life. Before I go to sleep tonight I give my word to...

_____
#1

_____
#2

_____
#3

_____
#4

_____
#5

_____

"Never was anything great achieved without danger."
~Niccolo' Machiavelli

FEBRUARY 15

Today, I am absolutely committed to Be, Do and Have more in my life. Before I go to sleep tonight I give my word to...

#1

#2

#3

#4

#5

"The moment you decide that what you know is more important than what you have been taught to believe, you will have shifted gears in your quest for abundance. Success comes from within, not from without."
~Ralph Waldo Emerson

FEBRUARY 16

Today, I am absolutely committed to Be, Do and Have more in my life. Before I go to sleep tonight I give my word to...

_____
#1

_____
#2

_____
#3

_____
#4

_____
#5

_____

"People love to share their fear, doubt and uncertainty so you will join them in the doldrums of depression, anxiety and fear. Break free and challenge them to a brighter future." ~James Murphy

FEBRUARY 17

Today, I am absolutely committed to Be, Do and Have more in my life. Before I go to sleep tonight I give my word to...

#1

#2

#3

#4

#5

"I have learned that success is to be measured not so much by the position that one has reached in life as by the obstacles which he has overcome while trying to succeed."
~Booker T. Washington

FEBRUARY 18

Today, I am absolutely committed to Be, Do and Have more in my life. Before I go to sleep tonight I give my word to...

_____
#1

_____
#2

_____
#3

_____
#4

_____
#5

_____

"Stand guard at the doorway of your mind, for what allow to enter, influences who you are." ~James Murphy

FEBRUARY 19

Today, I am absolutely committed to Be, Do and Have more in my life. Before I go to sleep tonight I give my word to...

_____
#1

_____
#2

_____
#3

_____
#4

_____
#5

_____

"People rarely succeed unless they have fun in what they are doing." ~Dale Carnegie

FEBRUARY 20

Today, I am absolutely committed to Be, Do and Have more in my life. Before I go to sleep tonight I give my word to...

#1

#2

#3

#4

#5

"I want to do it because I want to do it. Women must try to do things as men have tried. When they fail, their failure must be but a challenge to others."
~Amelia Earhart

FEBRUARY 21

Today, I am absolutely committed to Be, Do and Have more in my life. Before I go to sleep tonight I give my word to...

#1

#2

#3

#4

#5

"Success is a little like wrestling a gorilla. You don't quit when you are tired. You quit when the gorilla is tired."
~Robert Strauss

FEBRUARY 22

Today, I am absolutely committed to Be, Do and Have more in my life. Before I go to sleep tonight I give my word to...

#1

#2

#3

#4

#5

"There are many aspects to success; material wealth is only one component...But success also includes good health, energy and enthusiasm for life, fulfilling relationships, creative freedom, emotional and psychological stability, a sense of well being, and peace of mind." ~Deepak Chopra

FEBRUARY 23

Today, I am absolutely committed to Be, Do and Have more in my life. Before I go to sleep tonight I give my word to...

_____
#1

_____
#2

_____
#3

_____
#4

_____
#5

_____

"Peace and Love." ~Steven Goldfarb

FEBRUARY 24

Today, I am absolutely committed to Be, Do and Have more in my life. Before I go to sleep tonight I give my word to...

#1

#2

#3

#4

#5

"Success means we go to sleep at night knowing that our talents and abilities were used in a way that served others." ~Marianne Williamson

FEBRUARY 25

Today, I am absolutely committed to Be, Do and Have more in my life. Before I go to sleep tonight I give my word to...

_____
#1

_____

_____
#2

_____

_____
#3

_____

_____
#4

_____

_____
#5

_____

"Don't mistake activity with achievement."
~Coach John Wooden

FEBRUARY 26

Today, I am absolutely committed to Be, Do and Have more in my life. Before I go to sleep tonight I give my word to...

_____
#1

_____
#2

_____
#3

_____
#4

_____
#5

_____

"Rich people have small TV's and big libraries, and poor people have small libraries and big TV's."
~Zig Ziglar

FEBRUARY 27

Today, I am absolutely committed to Be, Do and Have more in my life. Before I go to sleep tonight I give my word to...

_____
#1

_____
#2

_____
#3

_____
#4

_____
#5

_____

"Get FIRED UP!" ~Mark Bible

FEBRUARY 28

Today, I am absolutely committed to Be, Do and Have more in my life. Before I go to sleep tonight I give my word to...

_____
#1

_____
#2

_____
#3

_____
#4

_____
#5

_____

"You have my word and I have my word."
~Kabral "the Genie" Sharpe

IN FEBRUARY I CREATED MORE...

MARCH 1

Today, I am absolutely committed to Be, Do and Have more in my life. Before I go to sleep tonight I give my word to...

#1

#2

#3

#4

#5

"If you care about what you do and work hard at it, there isn't anything you can't do if you want to."
~Jim Henson

MARCH 2

Today, I am absolutely committed to Be, Do and Have more in my life. Before I go to sleep tonight I give my word to...

#1

#2

#3

#4

#5

"In the greatest story ever told, which is your life, remember that you are the hero."   ~James Murphy

MARCH 3

Today, I am absolutely committed to Be, Do and Have more in my life. Before I go to sleep tonight I give my word to...

#1

#2

#3

#4

#5

"There is no failure except in no longer trying."
~Elbert Hubbard

MARCH 4

Today, I am absolutely committed to Be, Do and Have more in my life. Before I go to sleep tonight I give my word to...

_____
#1

_____
#2

_____
#3

_____
#4

_____
#5

_____

"To succeed in life, you need three things: a wish bone, a back bone and a funny bone."   ~Reba McEntire

MARCH 5

Today, I am absolutely committed to Be, Do and Have more in my life. Before I go to sleep tonight I give my word to...

#1

#2

#3

#4

#5

"Success is...knowing your purpose in life, growing to reach your maximum potential and sowing seeds that benefit others."   ~John C. Maxwell

MARCH 6

Today, I am absolutely committed to Be, Do and Have more in my life. Before I go to sleep tonight I give my word to...

#1

#2

#3

#4

#5

"Vision without execution is hallucination."
~Henry Ford

MARCH 7

Today, I am absolutely committed to Be, Do and Have more in my life. Before I go to sleep tonight I give my word to...

#1

#2

#3

#4

#5

"To balance the chaos in life around you, connect daily to the quiet place within you." ~James Murphy

MARCH 8

Today, I am absolutely committed to Be, Do and Have more in my life. Before I go to sleep tonight I give my word to...

#1

#2

#3

#4

#5

"To be independent of public opinion is the first formal condition of achieving anything great."
~George Hegel

MARCH 9

Today, I am absolutely committed to Be, Do and Have more in my life. Before I go to sleep tonight I give my word to...

_____
#1

_____
#2

_____
#3

_____
#4

_____
#5

_____

"More than 500 of the most successful men this country has ever known, told the author their greatest successes came just one step beyond the point at which defeat had overtaken them."   ~Napolean Hill

MARCH 10

Today, I am absolutely committed to Be, Do and Have more in my life. Before I go to sleep tonight I give my word to...

#1

#2

#3

#4

#5

"I can't tell you the key to success, but the key to failure is trying to please everyone."   ~Ed Sheeran

MARCH 11

Today, I am absolutely committed to Be, Do and Have more in my life. Before I go to sleep tonight I give my word to...

#1

#2

#3

#4

#5

"In order for something new to come into your life, a vacuum must first be created by giving something up, then find comfort in the emptiness until nature finds a way for your request to be filled."   ~James Murphy

MARCH 12

Today, I am absolutely committed to Be, Do and Have more in my life. Before I go to sleep tonight I give my word to...

_____
#1

_____
#2

_____
#3

_____
#4

_____
#5

_____

"Doing the best at this moment puts you in the best place for the next moment."   ~Oprah Winfrey

MARCH 13

Today, I am absolutely committed to Be, Do and Have more in my life. Before I go to sleep tonight I give my word to...

_____
#1

_____
#2

_____
#3

_____
#4

_____
#5

_____

"The thermometer of success is merely the jealousy of the malcontents." ~Salvador Dali'

MARCH 14

Today, I am absolutely committed to Be, Do and Have more in my life. Before I go to sleep tonight I give my word to...

_____
#1

_____
#2

_____
#3

_____
#4

_____
#5

_____

"It's failure that gives you the proper perspective on success."   ~Ellen DeGeneres

MARCH 15

Today, I am absolutely committed to Be, Do and Have more in my life. Before I go to sleep tonight I give my word to...

#1

#2

#3

#4

#5

"Understanding the difference between healthy striving and perfectionism is critical to laying down the shield and picking up your life. Perfectionism hampers success. In fact, it's often the path to depression, anxiety, addiction and live paralysis."   ~Brene' Brown

MARCH 16

Today, I am absolutely committed to Be, Do and Have more in my life. Before I go to sleep tonight I give my word to...

#1

#2

#3

#4

#5

"Each new day is a blank page in the diary of your life. The secret of success is in turning that diary into the best story you possibly can." ~Douglas Pagels

MARCH 17

Today, I am absolutely committed to Be, Do and Have more in my life. Before I go to sleep tonight I give my word to...

#1

#2

#3

#4

#5

"Decide what you want to be...Pay the price...and be what you want to be."   ~John Andreas Widtoe

MARCH 18

Today, I am absolutely committed to Be, Do and Have more in my life. Before I go to sleep tonight I give my word to...

#1

#2

#3

#4

#5

"Persistence, the breakfast of champions."
~James Murphy

MARCH 19

Today, I am absolutely committed to Be, Do and Have more in my life. Before I go to sleep tonight I give my word to...

#1

#2

#3

#4

#5

"Whosoever desires constant success must change his conduct with the times."   ~Niccolo' Machiavelli

MARCH 20

Today, I am absolutely committed to Be, Do and Have more in my life. Before I go to sleep tonight I give my word to...

_____
#1

_____
#2

_____
#3

_____
#4

_____
#5

_____

"The victim mindset dilutes the human potential. By not accepting personal responsibility for our circumstances, we greatly reduce our power to change them." ~Steve Maraboli

MARCH 21

Today, I am absolutely committed to Be, Do and Have more in my life. Before I go to sleep tonight I give my word to...

#1

#2

#3

#4

#5

"No one gets what they hope, wish or have an intention for, they get what their thoughts and actions lead the towards." ~ James Murphy

MARCH 22

Today, I am absolutely committed to Be, Do and Have more in my life. Before I go to sleep tonight I give my word to...

#1

#2

#3

#4

#5

"You must expect great things from yourself before you can do them." ~Michael Jordan

MARCH 23

Today, I am absolutely committed to Be, Do and Have more in my life. Before I go to sleep tonight I give my word to...

#1

#2

#3

#4

#5

"The roughest roads often lead to the top."
~Christina Aguilera

MARCH 24

Today, I am absolutely committed to Be, Do and Have more in my life. Before I go to sleep tonight I give my word to...

#1

#2

#3

#4

#5

"You may be disappointed if you fail, but you are doomed if you don't try." ~Beverly Sills

MARCH 25

Today, I am absolutely committed to Be, Do and Have more in my life. Before I go to sleep tonight I give my word to...

#1

#2

#3

#4

#5

"Define and find a purposeful way to live in every moment, not a lifestyle to live." ~James Murphy

MARCH 26

Today, I am absolutely committed to Be, Do and Have more in my life. Before I go to sleep tonight I give my word to...

#1

#2

#3

#4

#5

"The test of success is not what you do when you are on top. Success is how high you bounce when you hit the bottom." ~George S. Patton

MARCH 27

Today, I am absolutely committed to Be, Do and Have more in my life. Before I go to sleep tonight I give my word to...

#1

#2

#3

#4

#5

"Men (and women) are born to succeed, not to fail."
~Henry David Thoreau

MARCH 28

Today, I am absolutely committed to Be, Do and Have more in my life. Before I go to sleep tonight I give my word to...

_____
#1

_____
#2

_____
#3

_____
#4

_____
#5

_____

"Failure should be our teacher, not our undertaker. Failure is delay, not defeat. It is a temporary detour, not a dead end. Failure is something we can avoid only by saying nothing, doing nothing and being nothing."
~Denis Waitley

MARCH 29

Today, I am absolutely committed to Be, Do and Have more in my life. Before I go to sleep tonight I give my word to...

#1

#2

#3

#4

#5

"Don't worry about being perfect or pleasing others. Stay focused and act on being faithful to your truth."
~James Murphy

MARCH 30

Today, I am absolutely committed to Be, Do and Have more in my life. Before I go to sleep tonight I give my word to...

_____
#1

_____
#2

_____
#3

_____
#4

_____
#5

_____

"All the time you're saying to yourself, 'I could do that, but I won't,'-- is just another way of saying that you can't."
~Richard Feynman

MARCH 31

Today, I am absolutely committed to Be, Do and Have more in my life. Before I go to sleep tonight I give my word to...

#1

#2

#3

#4

#5

"The road to success is dotted with many tempting parking spaces." ~Will Rogers

IN MARCH, I CREATED MORE...

APRIL 1

Today, I am absolutely committed to Be, Do and Have more in my life. Before I go to sleep tonight I give my word to...

#1

#2

#3

#4

#5

"The whole secret of a successful life is to find out what is one's destiny to do, and then do it." ~Henry Ford

APRIL 2

Today, I am absolutely committed to Be, Do and Have more in my life. Before I go to sleep tonight I give my word to...

#1

#2

#3

#4

#5

"The secret is to fake it until you make it by acting as if... Act as if you are successful, wealthy, happy and fulfilled inside! The outside world will follow your lead."
~James Murphy

APRIL 3

Today, I am absolutely committed to Be, Do and Have more in my life. Before I go to sleep tonight I give my word to...

#1

#2

#3

#4

#5

"The merit of all things lies in their difficulty."
~Alexandre Dumas

APRIL 4

Today, I am absolutely committed to Be, Do and Have more in my life. Before I go to sleep tonight I give my word to...

#1

#2

#3

#4

#5

"Nearly only counts in horseshoes and hand grenades."
~Neil Gaiman

APRIL 5

Today, I am absolutely committed to Be, Do and Have more in my life. Before I go to sleep tonight I give my word to...

#1
_____

#2
_____

#3
_____

#4
_____

#5
_____

"Fortune sides with him who dares."
~Virgil

APRIL 6

Today, I am absolutely committed to Be, Do and Have more in my life. Before I go to sleep tonight I give my word to...

#1

#2

#3

#4

#5

"If you have a dream, don't just sit there. Gather courage to believe that you can succeed and leave no stone unturned to make it a reality."

~Roopleen

APRIL 7

Today, I am absolutely committed to Be, Do and Have more in my life. Before I go to sleep tonight I give my word to...

_____
#1

_____
#2

_____
#3

_____
#4

_____
#5

_____

"Time never flies by faster than one day at a time. Each day carries opportunity, will you step up and take it?"
~James Murphy

APRIL 8

Today, I am absolutely committed to Be, Do and Have more in my life. Before I go to sleep tonight I give my word to...

#1

#2

#3

#4

#5

"There are no secrets to success; don't waste time looking for them. Success is the result of perfection, hard work, learning from failure, loyalty to those for whom you work and persistence." ~Colin Powell

APRIL 9

Today, I am absolutely committed to Be, Do and Have more in my life. Before I go to sleep tonight I give my word to...

_____
#1

_____
#2

_____
#3

_____
#4

_____
#5

_____

"Don't let what you cannot do interfere with what you can do." ~John Wooden

APRIL 10

Today, I am absolutely committed to Be, Do and Have more in my life. Before I go to sleep tonight I give my word to...

_____
#1

_____
#2

_____
#3

_____
#4

_____
#5

_____

"From the day you were conceived, you were never a victim. The miracle of the human experience is love, learning and helping others." ~James Murphy

APRIL 11

Today, I am absolutely committed to Be, Do and Have more in my life. Before I go to sleep tonight I give my word to...

_____
#1

_____
#2

_____
#3

_____
#4

_____
#5

_____

"I was taught to strive not because there were any guarantees of success but because the act of striving is in itself the only way to keep faith with life."
~Madeleine Albright

APRIL 12

Today, I am absolutely committed to Be, Do and Have more in my life. Before I go to sleep tonight I give my word to...

#1

#2

#3

#4

#5

"Do not sit still; start moving now. In the beginning, you may not go in the direction you want, but as long as you are moving, you are creating alternatives and possibilities." ~Rodolfo Costa

APRIL 13

Today, I am absolutely committed to Be, Do and Have more in my life. Before I go to sleep tonight I give my word to...

#1

#2

#3

#4

#5

"The line between failure and success is so fine...that we are often on the line and do not know it."
~Elbert Hubbard

APRIL 14

Today, I am absolutely committed to Be, Do and Have more in my life. Before I go to sleep tonight I give my word to...

#1

#2

#3

#4

#5

"Gratitude for things you have are a great is nice, but the true power of gratitude lies in your problems. Be grateful for your problems for they are here to show you where you need to put your energy to grow and succeed."
~James Murphy

APRIL 15

Today, I am absolutely committed to Be, Do and Have more in my life. Before I go to sleep tonight I give my word to...

_____
#1

_____
#2

_____
#3

_____
#4

_____
#5

_____

"You have succeeded in life when all you really WANT is only what you really NEED."   ~Vernon Howard

APRIL 16

Today, I am absolutely committed to Be, Do and Have more in my life. Before I go to sleep tonight I give my word to...

#1

#2

#3

#4

#5

"Success is not obtained over night. It comes in installments; you get a little bit today, a little bit tomorrow until the whole package is given out. The day you procrastinate, you lost that day's success."

~Israelmore Ayivor

APRIL 17

Today, I am absolutely committed to Be, Do and Have more in my life. Before I go to sleep tonight I give my word to...

_____
#1

_____
#2

_____
#3

_____
#4

_____
#5

_____

"...it is well known that a vital ingredient of success is not knowing that what you're attempting can't be done."
~Terry Pratchett

APRIL 18

Today, I am absolutely committed to Be, Do and Have more in my life. Before I go to sleep tonight I give my word to...

#1

#2

#3

#4

#5

"The secret of success is constancy of purpose."
~Benjamin Disraeli

APRIL 19

Today, I am absolutely committed to Be, Do and Have more in my life. Before I go to sleep tonight I give my word to...

_____
#1

_____
#2

_____
#3

_____
#4

_____
#5

_____

"You only have to do a very few things right in your life so long as you don't do too many things wrong."
~Warren Buffett

APRIL 20

Today, I am absolutely committed to Be, Do and Have more in my life. Before I go to sleep tonight I give my word to...

#1

#2

#3

#4

#5

"What seems to us as bitter trials are often blessings in disguise." ~Oscar Wilde

APRIL 21

Today, I am absolutely committed to Be, Do and Have more in my life. Before I go to sleep tonight I give my word to...

_____
#1

_____
#2

_____
#3

_____
#4

_____
#5

_____

"Running is a whole and complete experience. I love running through the pain until your legs go numb, the mind stops spinning and finds calm, your breathing becomes a rhythmic song, your heart finds peace and you become one with God and nature. That is how to complete a 100-Mile race."   ~James Murphy

APRIL 22

Today, I am absolutely committed to Be, Do and Have more in my life. Before I go to sleep tonight I give my word to...

#1

#2

#3

#4

#5

"Accepting oneself does not preclude an attempt to become better."   ~Flannery O'Connor

APRIL 23

Today, I am absolutely committed to Be, Do and Have more in my life. Before I go to sleep tonight I give my word to...

#1

#2

#3

#4

#5

"Fear can only live in the dark. Bring along your flashlight and let's have a look under the bed. Hey, there's nothing there but an unfocused imagination!"
~James Murphy

APRIL 24

Today, I am absolutely committed to Be, Do and Have more in my life. Before I go to sleep tonight I give my word to...

#1

#2

#3

#4

#5

"Your success and happiness lie in you."
~Helen Keller

APRIL 25

Today, I am absolutely committed to Be, Do and Have more in my life. Before I go to sleep tonight I give my word to...

#1

#2

#3

#4

#5

"Don't be afraid of failure. This is the way to succeed."
~LeBron James

APRIL 26

Today, I am absolutely committed to Be, Do and Have more in my life. Before I go to sleep tonight I give my word to...

#1

#2

#3

#4

#5

"Be yourself; everyone else is already taken."
~Oscar Wilde

APRIL 27

Today, I am absolutely committed to Be, Do and Have more in my life. Before I go to sleep tonight I give my word to...

_____
#1

_____
#2

_____
#3

_____
#4

_____
#5

_____

"No one can make you feel inferior without your consent." ~Eleanor Roosevelt

APRIL 28

Today, I am absolutely committed to Be, Do and Have more in my life. Before I go to sleep tonight I give my word to...

#1

#2

#3

#4

#5

"Live as if you were to die tomorrow. Learn is if you were to live forever." ~Mahatma Gandhi

APRIL 29

Today, I am absolutely committed to Be, Do and Have more in my life. Before I go to sleep tonight I give my word to...

#1

#2

#3

#4

#5

"Darkness cannot drive our darkness; only light can do that. Hate cannot drive our hate; only love can do that."
~Martin Luther King, Jr.

APRIL 30

Today, I am absolutely committed to Be, Do and Have more in my life. Before I go to sleep tonight I give my word to...

#1

#2

#3

#4

#5

"There are only two ways to live your life. One is though nothing is a miracle. The other is as though everything is a miracle." ~Albert Einstein

IN APRIL, I CREATED MORE...

MAY 1

Today, I am absolutely committed to Be, Do and Have more in my life. Before I go to sleep tonight I give my word to...

#1

#2

#3

#4

#5

"I have not failed. I've just found 10,000 ways that won't work." ~Thomas A Edison

MAY 2

Today, I am absolutely committed to Be, Do and Have more in my life. Before I go to sleep tonight I give my word to...

#1

#2

#3

#4

#5

"You have brains in your head. You have feet on your shoes. You can steer yourself in any direction you choose. You're on your own. And you know what you know. And YOU are the one who'll decide where to go..."

~Dr. Seuss

MAY 3

Today, I am absolutely committed to Be, Do and Have more in my life. Before I go to sleep tonight I give my word to...

_____
#1

_____
#2

_____
#3

_____
#4

_____
#5

_____

"Fairy tales are more than true: not because they tell us that dragons exist, but because they tell us that dragons can be beaten." ~Neil Gaiman

MAY 4

Today, I am absolutely committed to Be, Do and Have more in my life. Before I go to sleep tonight I give my word to...

#1

#2

#3

#4

#5

"This life is what you make it. No matter what, you're going to mess up sometimes; it's a universal truth. Just because you fail once, doesn't mean you're gonna fail at everything. Keep trying, hold on, and always, always, always believe in yourself. Keep your head high, keep your chin up, and most importantly, keep smiling, because life's a beautiful thing and there's much to smile about."

~Marilyn Monroe

MAY 5

Today, I am absolutely committed to Be, Do and Have more in my life. Before I go to sleep tonight I give my word to...

_____
#1

_____
#2

_____
#3

_____
#4

_____
#5

_____

"It's never too late to be what you might have been."
~George Eliot

MAY 6

Today, I am absolutely committed to Be, Do and Have more in my life. Before I go to sleep tonight I give my word to...

_____
#1

_____
#2

_____
#3

_____
#4

_____
#5

_____

"Everything you can imagine is real."
~Pablo Picasso

MAY 7

Today, I am absolutely committed to Be, Do and Have more in my life. Before I go to sleep tonight I give my word to...

_____
#1

_____
#2

_____
#3

_____
#4

_____
#5

_____

"There is no greater agony than bearing an untold story inside you." ~Maya Angelou

MAY 8

Today, I am absolutely committed to Be, Do and Have more in my life. Before I go to sleep tonight I give my word to...

#1

#2

#3

#4

#5

"Do what you can, with what you have, where you are."
~Theodore Roosevelt

MAY 9

Today, I am absolutely committed to Be, Do and Have more in my life. Before I go to sleep tonight I give my word to...

#1

#2

#3

#4

#5

"When one door of happiness closes, another opens; but often we look so long at the closed door that we don not see the one which has been opened for us."
~Helen Keller

MAY 10

Today, I am absolutely committed to Be, Do and Have more in my life. Before I go to sleep tonight I give my word to...

#1

#2

#3

#4

#5

"To the well-organized mind, death is but the next great adventure." ~J.K. Rowling

MAY 11

Today, I am absolutely committed to Be, Do and Have more in my life. Before I go to sleep tonight I give my word to...

_____
#1

_____
#2

_____
#3

_____
#4

_____
#5

_____

"Life isn't about finding yourself. Life is about creating yourself." ~George Bernard Shaw

MAY 12

Today, I am absolutely committed to Be, Do and Have more in my life. Before I go to sleep tonight I give my word to...

#1

#2

#3

#4

#5

"Success is not final, failure is not fatal: it is the courage to continue that counts."   ~Winston S. Churchill

MAY 13

Today, I am absolutely committed to Be, Do and Have more in my life. Before I go to sleep tonight I give my word to...

#1

#2

#3

#4

#5

"I believe that laughing is the best calorie burner. I believe in being strong when everything seems to be gong wrong. I believe that tomorrow is another day and I believe in miracles."   ~Audrey Hepburn

MAY 14

Today, I am absolutely committed to Be, Do and Have more in my life. Before I go to sleep tonight I give my word to...

_____
#1

_____
#2

_____
#3

_____
#4

_____
#5

_____

"You may say I'm a dreamer, but I'm not the only one. I hope someday you'll join us. And the world will be at one." ~John Lennon

MAY 15

Today, I am absolutely committed to Be, Do and Have more in my life. Before I go to sleep tonight I give my word to...

_____
#1

_____
#2

_____
#3

_____
#4

_____
#5

_____

"What you're supposed to do when you don't like a thing is change it. If you can't change it, change the way you think about it. Don't complain."   ~Maya Angelou

MAY 16

Today, I am absolutely committed to Be, Do and Have more in my life. Before I go to sleep tonight I give my word to...

#1

#2

#3

#4

#5

"And, when you want something, all the universe conspires in helping you to achieve it."
~Paul Coelho

MAY 17

Today, I am absolutely committed to Be, Do and Have more in my life. Before I go to sleep tonight I give my word to...

#1

#2

#3

#4

#5

"You can't live your life for other people. You've got to do what's right for you, even if it hurts some people you love." ~Nicholas Sparks

MAY 18

Today, I am absolutely committed to Be, Do and Have more in my life. Before I go to sleep tonight I give my word to...

_____
#1

_____
#2

_____
#3

_____
#4

_____
#5

_____

"Getting MORE of what you want is like grocery shopping. If you go in with a shopping list for healthy meals you'll leave with them. If you go in hungry without a list, you come out with a lot of junk food."
~James Murphy

MAY 19

Today, I am absolutely committed to Be, Do and Have more in my life. Before I go to sleep tonight I give my word to...

_____
#1

_____
#2

_____
#3

_____
#4

_____
#5

_____

"I can't go back to yesterday because I was a different person then."   ~Lewis Carroll

MAY 20

Today, I am absolutely committed to Be, Do and Have more in my life. Before I go to sleep tonight I give my word to...

#1

#2

#3

#4

#5

"Do what you feel in your hear to be right - for you'll be criticized anyway."   ~Eleanor Roosevelt

MAY 21

Today, I am absolutely committed to Be, Do and Have more in my life. Before I go to sleep tonight I give my word to...

_____
#1

_____
#2

_____
#3

_____
#4

_____
#5

_____

"When I despair, I remember that all through history the way of truth and love have always won."
~Mahatma Gandhi

MAY 22

Today, I am absolutely committed to Be, Do and Have more in my life. Before I go to sleep tonight I give my word to...

#1

#2

#3

#4

#5

"The only thing that really makes life exciting is the sense of adventure that comes from working your dreams into reality." ~James Murphy

MAY 23

Today, I am absolutely committed to Be, Do and Have more in my life. Before I go to sleep tonight I give my word to...

_____
#1

_____
#2

_____
#3

_____
#4

_____
#5

_____

"First they ignore you, then they ridicule you, then they fight you, and then you win."   ~Mahatma Gandhi

MAY 24

Today, I am absolutely committed to Be, Do and Have more in my life. Before I go to sleep tonight I give my word to...

#1

#2

#3

#4

#5

"Never doubt that a small group of thoughtful, committed, citizens can change the world. Indeed, it is the only thing that ever has."   ~Margaret Mead

MAY 25

Today, I am absolutely committed to Be, Do and Have more in my life. Before I go to sleep tonight I give my word to...

#1

#2

#3

#4

#5

"May you live every day of your life."
~Jonathan Swift

MAY 26

Today, I am absolutely committed to Be, Do and Have more in my life. Before I go to sleep tonight I give my word to...

#1

#2

#3

#4

#5

"Always do what you are afraid to do."
~Ralph Waldo Emerson

MAY 27

Today, I am absolutely committed to Be, Do and Have more in my life. Before I go to sleep tonight I give my word to...

_____
#1

_____
#2

_____
#3

_____
#4

_____
#5

_____

"Our lives begin to end the day we become silent about things that matter."   ~Martin Luther King, Jr.

MAY 28

Today, I am absolutely committed to Be, Do and Have more in my life. Before I go to sleep tonight I give my word to...

#1

#2

#3

#4

#5

"Talent hits the target no one else can hit. Genius hits a target no one else can see."   ~Arthur Schopenhauer

MAY 29

Today, I am absolutely committed to Be, Do and Have more in my life. Before I go to sleep tonight I give my word to...

_____
#1

_____
#2

_____
#3

_____
#4

_____
#5

_____

"Do not let the hero in your soul perish in the lonely frustration for the life you deserved and have never been able to reach. The world you desire can be won. It exists...it is real...it is possible...it is yours."

~Ayn Rand

MAY 30

Today, I am absolutely committed to Be, Do and Have more in my life. Before I go to sleep tonight I give my word to...

#1

#2

#3

#4

#5

"If my life is going to mean anything, I have to live it myself." ~Rick Riordan

MAY 31

Today, I am absolutely committed to Be, Do and Have more in my life. Before I go to sleep tonight I give my word to...

#1

#2

#3

#4

#5

"Do not go where the path may lead, go instead where there is no path and leave a trail."
~Ralph Waldo Emerson

IN MAY, I CREATED MORE...

JUNE 1

Today, I am absolutely committed to Be, Do and Have more in my life. Before I go to sleep tonight I give my word to...

_____
#1

_____
#2

_____
#3

_____
#4

_____
#5

_____

"If you can't fly then run, if you can't run then walk, if you can't walk then crawl, but whatever you do you have to keep moving forward."   ~Martin Luther King, Jr.

JUNE 2

Today, I am absolutely committed to Be, Do and Have more in my life. Before I go to sleep tonight I give my word to...

#1

#2

#3

#4

#5

"Today is the day to conquer whatever you fear or are procrastinating most. Boldly paint the next stroke on the masterpiece painting called your life."
~James Murphy

JUNE 3

Today, I am absolutely committed to Be, Do and Have more in my life. Before I go to sleep tonight I give my word to...

#1

#2

#3

#4

#5

"If you're reading this...Congratulations, you're alive. If that's not something to smile about, the I don't know what is." ~Chad Sugg

JUNE 4

Today, I am absolutely committed to Be, Do and Have more in my life. Before I go to sleep tonight I give my word to...

#1

#2

#3

#4

#5

"I am not sure exactly what heaven will be like, but I know that when we die and it comes time for God to jedge us, he will not ask, 'How many good things have you done in your life?' rather he will ask, 'How much love did you put into what you did?" ~Mother Teresa

JUNE 5

Today, I am absolutely committed to Be, Do and Have more in my life. Before I go to sleep tonight I give my word to...

_____
#1

_____
#2

_____
#3

_____
#4

_____
#5

_____

"When you have eliminated all which is possible, then whatever remains, however improbable, must be the truth." ~Arthur Conan Doyle

JUNE 6

Today, I am absolutely committed to Be, Do and Have more in my life. Before I go to sleep tonight I give my word to...

#1

#2

#3

#4

#5

"Turn your wounds into wisdom."
~Oprah Winfrey

JUNE 7

Today, I am absolutely committed to Be, Do and Have more in my life. Before I go to sleep tonight I give my word to...

#1

#2

#3

#4

#5

"I like living. I have sometimes been wildly, despairingly, acutely miserable, racked with sorrow; but through it all I still know quite certainly that just to be alive is a grand thing." ~Agatha Christie

JUNE 8

Today, I am absolutely committed to Be, Do and Have more in my life. Before I go to sleep tonight I give my word to...

#1

#2

#3

#4

#5

"None but ourselves can free our mind."
~Bob Marley

JUNE 9

Today, I am absolutely committed to Be, Do and Have more in my life. Before I go to sleep tonight I give my word to...

#1

#2

#3

#4

#5

"The world is indeed full of peril, and in it there are many dark places; but still there is much that is fair, and thought in all lands love is now mingled with grief, it grows perhaps the greater." ~J.R.R. Tolkien

JUNE 10

Today, I am absolutely committed to Be, Do and Have more in my life. Before I go to sleep tonight I give my word to...

_____
#1

_____
#2

_____
#3

_____
#4

_____
#5

_____

"Sometimes our light goes out, but it is blown again into instant flame by an encounter with another human being." ~Albert Schweitzer

JUNE 11

Today, I am absolutely committed to Be, Do and Have more in my life. Before I go to sleep tonight I give my word to...

#1

#2

#3

#4

#5

"It isn't what you have or who you are or where you are or what you are doing that makes you happy or unhappy. It is what you think about it." ~Dale Carnegie

JUNE 12

Today, I am absolutely committed to Be, Do and Have more in my life. Before I go to sleep tonight I give my word to...

#1

#2

#3

#4

#5

"Don't judge each day by the harvest you reap but by the seeds that you plant."   ~Robert Louis Stevenson

JUNE 13

Today, I am absolutely committed to Be, Do and Have more in my life. Before I go to sleep tonight I give my word to...

#1

#2

#3

#4

#5

"It's kind of fun to do the impossible."
~Walt Disney

JUNE 14

Today, I am absolutely committed to Be, Do and Have more in my life. Before I go to sleep tonight I give my word to...

#1

#2

#3

#4

#5

"A painter should begin every canvas with a wash of black, because all things in nature are dark except where exposed by the light." ~Leonardo da Vinci

JUNE 15

Today, I am absolutely committed to Be, Do and Have more in my life. Before I go to sleep tonight I give my word to...

#1

#2

#3

#4

#5

"The secret of health for both mind and body is not to mourn for the past, nor to worry about the future, but to live the present moment wisely and earnestly."
~Gautama Buddha

JUNE 16

Today, I am absolutely committed to Be, Do and Have more in my life. Before I go to sleep tonight I give my word to...

#1

#2

#3

#4

#5

"Pain is temporary. Quitting lasts forever."
~Lance Armstrong

JUNE 17

Today, I am absolutely committed to Be, Do and Have more in my life. Before I go to sleep tonight I give my word to...

_____
#1

_____
#2

_____
#3

_____
#4

_____
#5

_____

"Don't say you don't have enough time. You have exactly the same number of hours per day that were given to Helen Keller, Pasteur, Michaelangelo, Mother Teresa, Leonardo da Vinci, Thomas Jefferson and Albert Einstein." ~H. Jackson Brown, Jr.

JUNE 18

Today, I am absolutely committed to Be, Do and Have more in my life. Before I go to sleep tonight I give my word to...

#1

#2

#3

#4

#5

"You can focus on the darkness all around you or look up to see the shooting stars, distant planets and fabulous Milky Way." ~James Murphy

JUNE 19

Today, I am absolutely committed to Be, Do and Have more in my life. Before I go to sleep tonight I give my word to...

#1

#2

#3

#4

#5

"You see things; you say, 'Why?' But I dream things that never were; and I say 'Why not?'"
~George Bernard Shaw

JUNE 20

Today, I am absolutely committed to Be, Do and Have more in my life. Before I go to sleep tonight I give my word to...

#1

#2

#3

#4

#5

"The most important kind of freedom is to be what you really are. You trade in your reality for a role. You trade in your sense for an act. You give up your ability feel, and in exchange, put on a mask. There can't be any large-scale revolution until there's a personal revolution, on an individual lever. It's got to happen inside first."

~Jim Morrison

JUNE 21

Today, I am absolutely committed to Be, Do and Have more in my life. Before I go to sleep tonight I give my word to...

#1

#2

#3

#4

#5

"I do not fear death. I had been dead for billions and billions of years before I was born, and had not suffered the slightest inconvenience from it."

~Mark Twain

JUNE 22

Today, I am absolutely committed to Be, Do and Have more in my life. Before I go to sleep tonight I give my word to...

#1

#2

#3

#4

#5

"Live in the present, remember the past, and fear not the future, for it doesn't exist and never shall. There is only now." ~Christopher Paolini

JUNE 23

Today, I am absolutely committed to Be, Do and Have more in my life. Before I go to sleep tonight I give my word to...

#1

#2

#3

#4

#5

"Start writing, no matter what. The water doesn't start to flow until the faucet is turned on."   ~Louis L'Amour

JUNE 24

Today, I am absolutely committed to Be, Do and Have more in my life. Before I go to sleep tonight I give my word to...

_____
#1

_____
#2

_____
#3

_____
#4

_____
#5

_____

"The mind is its own place, and in itself can make a heaven of hell, a hell of heaven..."   ~John Milton

JUNE 25

Today, I am absolutely committed to Be, Do and Have more in my life. Before I go to sleep tonight I give my word to...

#1

#2

#3

#4

#5

"Even if you are on the right track, you'll get run over if you just sit there." ~Wil Rogers

JUNE 26

Today, I am absolutely committed to Be, Do and Have more in my life. Before I go to sleep tonight I give my word to...

#1

#2

#3

#4

#5

"The thing about growing up with Fred and George," said Ginny thoughtfully, "is that you sort of start thinking anything's possible if you've get enough nerve."

~J.K. Rowling

JUNE 27

Today, I am absolutely committed to Be, Do and Have more in my life. Before I go to sleep tonight I give my word to...

#1

#2

#3

#4

#5

"Courage is not the absence of fear, but rather the judgment that something else is more important than fear." ~Ambrose Redmoon

JUNE 28

Today, I am absolutely committed to Be, Do and Have more in my life. Before I go to sleep tonight I give my word to...

_____
#1

_____
#2

_____
#3

_____
#4

_____
#5

_____

What's the good of living if you don't try a few things?"
~Charles Schultz

JUNE 29

Today, I am absolutely committed to Be, Do and Have more in my life. Before I go to sleep tonight I give my word to...

#1

#2

#3

#4

#5

"Once the storm is over, you won't remember how you made it through, how you managed to survive. You won't be sure, whether the storm is really over. But one thing is certain. When you come out of the storm, you won't be the same person who walked in. That's what the storm is all about."   ~Haruki Murakami

JUNE 30

Today, I am absolutely committed to Be, Do and Have more in my life. Before I go to sleep tonight I give my word to...

_____
#1

_____
#2

_____
#3

_____
#4

_____
#5

_____

"Try a little harder to be a little better!"
~Gordon B. Hinckley

IN JUNE, I CREATED MORE...

TAKE A MOMENT AND REFLECT ON THE LAST 6 MONTHS...

1. WHO HAVE YOU BECOME?
2. WHAT HAVE YOU BUILT & CREATED?
3. WHAT HAVE YOU LEARNED?
4. HOW HAVE YOU CHANGED?
5. WHO HAVE YOU INSPIRED?
6. WHY DO YOU WANT TO CONTINUE?

**FOCUS -- BUILD -- CREATE -- ACHIEVE -- INSPIRE
TO YOUR CONTINUED SUCCESS, JAMES**

"IT IS NOT THE CRITIC WHO COUNTS; NOT THE MAN WHO POINTS OUT HOW THE STRONG MAN STUMBLES, OR WHERE THE DOER OF DEEDS COULD HAVE DONE THEM BETTER. THE CREDIT BELONGS TO THE MAN WHO IS ACTUALLY IN THE ARENA, WHOSE FACE IS MARRED BY DUST AND SWEAT AND BLOOD; WHO STRIVES VALIANTLY; WHO ERRS, WHO COMES SHORT AGAIN AND AGAIN, BECAUSE THERE IS NO EFFORT WITHOUT ERROR AND SHORTCOMING; BUT WHO DOES ACTUALLY STRIVE TO DO THE DEEDS; WHO KNOWS GREAT ENTHUSIASMS, THE GREAT DEVOTIONS; WHO SPENDS HIMSELF IN A WORTHY CAUSE; WHO AT THE BEST KNOWS IN THE END THE TRIUMPH OF HIGH ACHIEVEMENT, AND WHO AT THE WORST, IF HE FAILS, AT LEAST FAILS WHILE DARING GREATLY, SO THAT HIS PLACE SHALL NEVER BE WITH THOSE COLD AND TIMID SOULS WHO NEITHER KNOW VICTORY NOR DEFEAT."

~THEODORE ROOSEVELT

CONGRATULATIONS!!!

TAKE A MOMENT AND APPRECIATE YOUR HARD WORK, DEDICATION & HONORING YOUR WORD!

ORDER:

MORE...
VOLUME II
JULY-DECEMBER

WWW.EVOLUTIONFORSUCCESS.COM
~OR~
CALL JAMES MURPHY
(919) 745-7569
AND RECEIVE YOUR COPY
IMMEDIATELY!

ASK ABOUT THE **'SUCCESS-NOW'** SESSION THAT HAS BEEN RESERVED JUST FOR YOU!

JAMES M MURPHY
AUTHOR, SPEAKER, EXECUTIVE BUSINESS COACH
www.evolutionforsuccess.com
www.30DaysforSuccess.com
www.businessmarketingforsuccess.com
james@evolutionforsuccess.com

(919) 792-0085

James M Murphy has been an Executive Business & Life Coach for the last 16 years. James began with Anthony Robbins Companies as a Peak Performance Results Coach working with entrepreneurs, business owners and executives in 1999.

Through his incredible immersion experience, James' extensive coaching experience dwarfs most coaches in the market today. After conducting over 25,000 sessions, he is a master in the psychology of time management, the entrepreneurial mindset, emotional mastery, goal setting, focus and productivity, problem resolution, communication, money, health and relationships.

James has expanded his skills to include working with clients deeper emotional issues to include release of anxiety, overwhelm, fears and phobias. He is a Master Practitioner of Neuro Linguistic Programming (NLP), Time Line Therapy™ and Hypnosis.

James also developed the Sure Hire Employee Evaluation tool which has saved his clients tens of thousands of dollars by hiring the right employees the first time. It is a one of a kind assessment cross referencing the DiSC™ Behavioral Assessment, NLP Meta programs, and Values (emotional drivers) Psychology.

Looking for a Keynote Speaker?

James has given keynote presentations for companies including General Mills, Dish Network, Walgreens, Robert Half International, NC State and the Resource Coaching Academy.

The Power of Purpose: the #1 Quality of a Leader

Summary of Session:

This program will bring energy, passion and purpose back into a corporation. It provides a simple foundation of Success principles to motivate and engage employees. The company all the way down to the individuals Purpose will be defined. A new empowered corporate mindset will be employed and the 3 Finish lines to any goal will be presented in a fun, engaging and dynamic way. My messages speak to every person in the company regardless of position.

Other Keynotes include:

Stumbling to Stepping Stones: **People without Purpose, Perish.**
Are you waking up in the morning stuck, unmotivated, feeling deep desire for something 'more' but don't know what? Purpose is what you are looking for. What are the 3 factors or a Purposeful Life? Leave this session with your own answer to the question, "What is my purpose in life?"

F.O.C.U.S. and Motivation: *The Cycle of Success and Achievement*

Are you or your friends stuck in a rut? Have they lost their mojo and desire? Keeping yourself and others engaged in the Cycle of Success is critical. Learn how to stay happier, more satisfied and engaged in your work. The Motivational Football approach will keep you confident and empowered.

Creating Conversation: *The Power of Language for Persuasion, Purpose and Profits*

One of the biggest reasons for letting a person go in business is poor communication. Powerful, purposeful communication is essential for managing, selling and effective leadership. Discover how to communicate more effectively consciously and unconsciously with others. Learn how to displace resistance to new ideas and find more ways of effectively creating change through speech.

Accelerated Learning: *Producing the Highest Grades in the Best Time*

Have you ever felt there had to be an easier way to study? Do you suffer from test anxiety and undue stress. Unfortunately, we were never taught how to use our brain effectively to excel in school. Learn cutting edge tools, processes and exercises guaranteed to raise your grades at least one level in this incredible breakthrough session.

Creating Conversation: *The Power of Language for Persuasion, Purpose and Profits*
One of the biggest reasons for letting a person go in business is poor communication. Powerful, purposeful communication is essential for managing, selling and effective leadership. Discover how to communicate more effectively consciously and unconsciously with others. Learn how to displace resistance to new ideas and find more ways of effectively creating change through speech.

The Power of Money: *3 Guiding Principles for Security, Safety and Responsible Living*
Doe you get scared when the subject of money comes up? Are you afraid of managing what you have? Are you afraid of losing it all? Discover the 3 simple, fundamental steps to create all of the financial security, safety and abundance you desire. Money Mastery is Magical.

From Madness to Meditation: *Stress Release for Health, Energy and a Vibrant Life*
Are you stressed? Does tension wrack your mind, body and spirit? Meditation has been proven to boost energy, release tension and stress and increase health and wellness. Learn the two reasons to meditate, how to 'meditate on the light', and improve your life. It is easy, simple and anyone can do it. Stay calm and carry on.

Call now for more information on how you can bring James into your company for a powerful day of training!

(919) 792-0085 Office
(919) 745-7569 Cell
james@evolutionforsuccess.com

www.evolutionforsuccess.com
www.30DaysforSuccess.com
www.businessmarketingforsuccess.com

CALL NOW

and set up your complimentary

'Success-Now' Session

and discover how personal one-on-one Executive Business Coaching can Accelerate your Life and Business to the next level!